Introduction by W. Terrence Gordon

This essay, reprinted from *Explorations* 3, Toronto: University of Toronto Press, August 1954, pages 120-126, complements McLuhan's contribution to the previous volume of *Explorations*, Notes on the Media as Art Forms. And so, he opens his discussion of media as political forms by heralding James Joyce's "optophone principle in art" as "the key for future literary *and* social education." (my emphasis—WTG) The principle stems from a technology: "The optophone is an instrument for turning images into sounds." As such, it is a medium for dealphabetizing retribalized man, for coping with the "political crisis with the passing of the press into the entertainment limbo, and with the rise of TV as a political shaper." —WTG

New Media as Political Forms

For the lineal procedure of individual awareness, Joyce, in his last work, substituted an everyday roundabout with intrusions from above and below. For those locked in the metallic and rectilinear embrace of the printed page, Joyce appears as a surrealist magician or clown. But his optophone principle in art provides the key for future literary and social education. The optophone is an instrument for turning images into sounds. Surrounded by a vast new imagery, technological man has yet to learn how to interpret this imagery verbally or socially. Until he learns its language it will continue to act on him like the new liquid meat tenderizers. In the *Wake* Joyce provided the sounds which are the magic key to the new technological visual environment. More than that, these sounds are both acoustically and semantically continuous with the linguistic activity of the race. The *Wake* may take a few months to get acquainted with, but it represents a great short-cut to the encyclopedic arts and sciences of our century. It is the sheer quantity of information which has alienated us from political and social reality. The large city isolates the individual citizen, but the multi-cultural perspectives of the press have isolated the human spirit itself from any milieu.

A decisive instance of this isolation is the popular sleuth of detective fiction. Whether it be Holmes or Marlowe the sleuth is an alienated man, but he is one who uses the communication networks of the metropolis as a kind of musical instrument. The appeal of detective stories is not least in the power of the sleuth to control the city as an instrument of expression. He turns the city into poetry.

What Joyce has shown us is how to do for the whole of existence what the sleuth does with the keyboard of the city. Today we are compelled by the quantity of available social and political facts to learn a new visual language for swiftly mastering the inner dynamics by the outer carapace of facts.

Perhaps nothing more bespeaks the hypnotic and irrational pressure of the book-page than the scant attention it has received as a form. In the 16th century it required an effort to read print comparable to the effort today exerted to master symphonic scores or mathematical pictograms. Moreover a passage of Greene, Lyly, or Nashe is not prose in the 18th or 19th century sense. The focus of attention has to be readjusted for changes of tone and attitude in every sentence. Print had not yet imposed its massive mechanical weight to level off the oral and colloquial features of prose. Even punctuation was not for the reading eye but the speaking voice—a fact lost on the 19th century editors of Shakespeare. The triumphs of 20th century editing of Shakespeare have mainly consisted in abandoning the habits of rigid perspective induced by three centuries of print-hypnosis. Print is an ill master for those who are unaware of the precise nature and scope of its power. The printed word is no longer a means of testing reality. *Caveat emptor.*

The modern movie camera resembles Elizabethan prose in its demands of agility and multiple mental focus. *Vogue* recently printed an essay by an English novelist who confessed that he was mostly unable to follow the development of movie narrative and characterization and that he had to rely on his less bookish wife to interpret the action to him.

Rosamond Tuve in a recent book on George Herbert makes it her theme that the metaphysical poets, so congenial to our century, typically found their novel effects in the transfer of traditional pictorial imagery to the new printed page. Hers is no friendly analysis. In 1600 print was in the ascendant and the old pictorial 'Bibles of the Poor,' painted cloths, dumb shows and popular spectacles were in decline. Today the reverse process obtains. At the equilibrium point in these two processes the seventeenth century metaphysical poets shot up into favorable view once more. We shared with them for twenty years a bi-focal vision of the interfusion of two media.

At the end of the 18 th century Whiter, an Anglican clergyman, anticipated much 20th century critical appreciation of Shakespeare by studying the imagery of his plays. One of his observations was that Shakespeare in *Antony and Cleopatra* or *The Tempest*, for example, brought verbally to the ordinary man the gorgeous scenic virtuosities of the Jacobean court masque.

In *Spirit of the Age* (1825) William Hazlitt summed up a century of romantic revolt and experiment in his comments on the relation between books and painting:

> Book-learning, the accumulation of wordy common-places, the gaudy pretensions of poetical fiction, had enfeebled and perverted our eye for nature. The study of the fine arts, which came into fashion about forty years ago, and was then first considered as a polite accomplishment, would tend imperceptibly to restore it. Painting is essentially an imitative art; it cannot subsist for a moment on empty generalities: the critic, therefore, who had been used to this sort of substantial entertainment, would be disposed to read poetry with the eye of a connoisseur, would be little captivated with smooth, polished, unmeaning periods, and would turn with double eagerness and relish to the force and precision of individual details, transferred, as it were, to the page from the canvas. Thus an admirer of Teniers or Hobbima might think little of the pastoral sketches of Pope or Goldsmith; even Thomson describes not so much the naked object as what he sees in his mind's eye, surrounded and glowing with the mild, bland, genial vapours of his brain: — but the adept in Dutch interiors . . . must find in Mr. Crabbe a man after his own heart. He is the very thing itself; he paints in words instead of colours. . . . All the rest might be found in a newspaper, an old magazine, or a county-register.

George Crabbe was Lord Tennyson's favorite narrative poet. And the early Tennyson was a radical experimenter in picturesque painting technique. It may well have been Arnold whose criticism turned English literary attention away for a few decades from an inclusive consciousness of the techniques in the arts. From Chaucer to Tennyson it would be hard to find a poet who was not an eager student of the non-literary culture of his own day. But since English became a university subject (in the past fifty years or less) it has been customary not only to study poetry and letters without reference to technique and effect but in isolation from the other arts and sciences. It has been observed that any crisis in a culture, an organization, or a person calls for a great extension of the internal and external modes of communication. Precisely the reverse of this has occurred in the area of book-culture today.

This fact explains a good deal of the current helplessness in literary circles with regard to illiteracy and the new media. The study of the classics earlier disappeared in the same fashion. Writing in *Encounter* (April, 1954), Auden discusses 'The Word and the Machine'. Poets today, he says, envy 'not the rich or the powerful but the scientists, doctors, machine designers, etc., for whose happiness our age seems designed as earlier ages were designed for great landowners, for these people enjoy the satisfaction both of meaningful work and of an unequivocal social position. When I am in the company of scientists, I feel like a curate who has strayed into a drawing-room full of dukes.'

A few years before, Mr. Auden's colleague Stephen Spender was wanly asking why, when he met a communist, did he feel so small? Both having failed in the thirties to find a satisfactory lyrical idiom to glorify the machine might now unite in the matter of dukes. Or doesn't it matter that the machine has now brought English noblemen to the pass of purveying homemade jam at the roadside? The fact of the matter is that Mr. Auden typifies our current failure to examine the forms of technology, past and present, as art forms. He concludes his essay:

> Is there something in the essential natures of the machine and the Word which makes them incompatible, so that at the slightest contact with the former the Word turns into lifeless words? Is even the mechanical printing press, but for which I would never have been able to read the books that formed my life, nor for that matter be writing this article now, an evil? Sometimes I have an uneasy suspicion that it is.

After four centuries of uncritical ebullience and commercial log-rolling it would seem to be safe to have a suspicion about the effects of print. Especially now that print has been knocked off its pedestal by other media. But it is still not too late to save some of the qualities of mind fostered by the printed page, provided we are prepared to note exactly what the limits of those qualities are and have been. Study of preliterate societies and manuscript cultures can give excellent indications of the merits and defects of book-culture. These in coordination with music and painting as technical forms of managing experience can in turn provide excellent clues for understanding the new pictorial media.

Sigfried Giedion has given exact procedures for how the modern painter or poet should conduct himself in the company of scientists: Adopt and adapt their discoveries to the uses of art. Why leave this solely to the distortions of the industrialist? Newton revolutionized the techniques of poetry and painting. Joyce encompasses Einstein but extends his pictographic formula to the entire world of language and consciousness. The tendency of the challengingly new to revoke and reinforce ancient disciplines never appeared more strikingly than in Joyce. Literature may have come to an end in 1870 but poetic, rhetoric and metaphysic have come increasingly alive since then.

One reason why the literate English world is so helpless in the presence of the new media is perhaps owing to England's having been so backward in 1500. The Wars of the Roses had delayed the impact of the Renaissance. In England alone that impact coincided with the arrival of the printing press. The cultural lopsidedness of a literary monopoly appears even more strikingly in New England in the 17 th century. But it needs to be stressed that printed culture is itself a triumph of the machine. And book-culture in England and America was *in its very format* a great incentive to the mechanization of society. The book-page is the first mass-produced machine product. This fact is as obvious to men of Mediterranean culture as the fact that backward communities are the oral libraries of the world's ancient cultures is obvious to archaeologists. Why should it be surprising that the most literate societies are the most mechanized? Why should literate men bemoan the mechanization of speech and gesture (radio and television) when it is precisely the mechanization of writing that made this development possible? Would it be too much to suggest that universal literacy is unfriendly to critical perception? With 25,000 and more new titles in English each year who is to note the significant, let alone 'the best that has been thought and said in the world'?

It is the almost total coverage of the globe in time and space that has rendered the book an increasingly obsolete form of communication. The slow movement of the eye along lines of type, the slow procession of items organized by the mind to fit into these endless horizontal columns, these procedures can't stand up to the pressures of instantaneous coverage of the earth.

The American Revolution occurred just when the newspaper was sufficiently a reality to be changing and extending surface transport. The American Government was the first to be founded on the concept of public opinion. Such a concept still seems bizarre in Canada. It was the new medium not of the book but the press which shaped the U.S.A. And this creates a political crisis with the passing of the press into the entertainment limbo, and with the rise of TV as a political shaper. But it has also been the typical mistake of literate cultures to regard entertainment as non-political. Russia made no such slip.

What is to be expected in the mainly non-literate India and China, countries which are in a position to by-pass literacy and proceed at once with radio and TV? These countries represent high cultures which are almost entirely oral and pictographic. Their rapport with TV far exceeds our own. If the new medium of the press gave a radical imprint to American politics, how much more might the new medium of TV be ordained to shape power patterns in the Orient? Should this occur, our own political structures, tied to print, would be quite unable to catch up. Russia provides some hints for this process. Enjoying the end products of our technology as regards industry, press, radio, and movie, it assumed them at a pre-industrial point in its own development, just as the Orient is in a position to assume endproducts of an even later stage of our development into an even earlier stage of its own. The dream-character of movie and TV realism would seem to be connaturally adjusted to 'the dreaming East'. The giant djinns of oriental fancy are pygmy-like in size and power compared even with the superhuman dimensions conferred by our own daily press and weekly magazines on nobody in particular. But even more, movie and TV have the almost uncontrollable power of inflating the most casually selected persons into million horse-powered entities. Men trained in book-culture are slow to assess these facts. Yet they will admit that even books, by and large, have been written by their reading publics. Authors have always been shaped by their potential publics.

But the new media are not 'authored' by single individuals any more than a modern newspaper. As the public of the new media increases the 'author' staff increases. Scott or Dickens could net a nation. But no single writer today can encompass more than a fragment of the available attention of the public. The media have transformed the public in many ways and the public goes on transforming the techniques and consciousness of the authors who would master it. The man who has something to say is the man who has mastered some segment of public awareness. He is capable of lighting up some dim, fusty corner of embryonic social consciousness. Formerly an author could do this by introspection, when he was essentially a member of society. Today when it is no longer possible to be sure of what being a member of society may involve, the 'author' has to bestir himself as much as any pollster. He lives in an unknown world of strange new components and effects.

In *Explorations Two* it was suggested that the new situation in the modern class-room is that the adolescent today does not need information. He is hopelessly overloaded with messages from the urban environment. The class-room no longer need typically perform the function of providing facts. It must above all provide techniques of recognition and discrimination. Reality-testing can no longer follow the linear, factual recital or statistical pattern. There is far too much reality for that. We are obliged to deal with reality in constellations and clusters or not at all. If politics and the citizen are to survive the new media, we must alter our entire sighting and range-finding apparatus, which is still oriented to the printed page alone.

Marshall McLuhan

New Media as Political Forms
Marshall McLuhan - Unbound (14)

ISBN: 1-58423-051-7
Library of Congress Control Number 2005927213

Marshall McLuhan Unbound Project Editors
Eric McLuhan, W. Terrence Gordon

Published in United States in October 2005 by
Gingko Press, Inc.
5768 Paradise Drive, Suite J • Corte Madera, CA 94925
(415) 924-9615 • Fax (415) 924-9608
email: books@gingkopress.com
http://www.gingkopress.com

Design, packaging and production: Die Gestalten Verlag, Berlin
Layout and Typography: onlab, Berlin
Fonts: *Dolly* by Underware, *Bullet* by House Industries
Production: Martin Bretschneider, Vinzenz Geppert
Art direction: Robert Klanten

Made in Germany